PETER PIPER'S ALPHABET

PETER PIPER'S PRACTICAL PRINCIPLES OF PLAIN AND PERFECT PRONUNCIATION

MANIFOLD MANIFESTATIONS MADE BY MARCIA BROWN

FOR A. C. M.

CHARLES SCRIBNER'S SONS NEW YORK

P-PREFACE

Peter Piper, without
Pretension to Precocity or
Profoundness, Puts Pen to
Paper to Produce these
Puzzling Pages,
Purposely to Please the
Palates of Pretty
Prattling Playfellows,
Proudly Presuming that with
Proper Penetration it will
Probably, and Perhaps
Positively, Prove a
Peculiarly Pleasant and
Profitable Path to Proper,
Plain and Precise
Pronunciation. He
Prays Parents to
Purchase this Playful
Performance, Partly to
Pay him for his
Patience and Pains;
Partly to Provide for the
Printers and Publishers; but
Principally to Prevent the
Pernicious Prevalence of
Perverse Pronunciation.

E-2.73 (CLD)
PRINTED IN THE UNITED STATES OF AMERICA
SBN 684-13128-5 (CLOTH)

ANDREW AIRPUMP asked his Aunt her Ailment:
Did Andrew Airpump ask his Aunt her Ailment?
If Andrew Airpump asked his Aunt her Ailment,
Where was the Ailment of Andrew Airpump's Aunt?

BILLY BUTTON bought a buttered Biscuit;
Did Billy Button buy a buttered Biscuit?
If Billy Button bought a buttered Biscuit,
Where's the buttered Biscuit Billy Button bought?

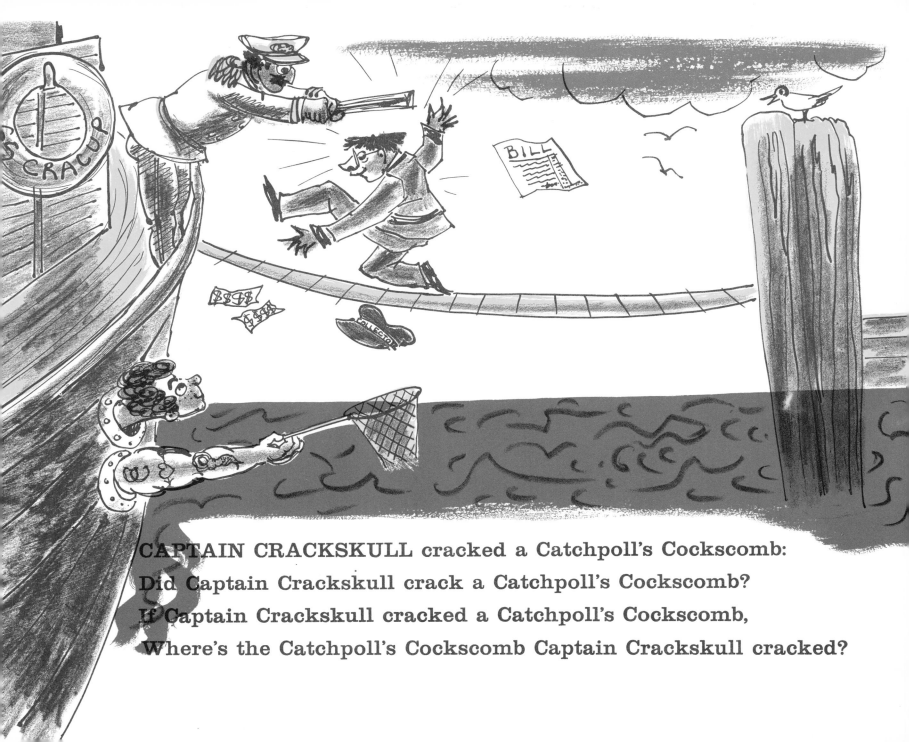

CAPTAIN CRACKSKULL cracked a Catchpoll's Cockscomb:
Did Captain Crackskull crack a Catchpoll's Cockscomb?
If Captain Crackskull cracked a Catchpoll's Cockscomb,
Where's the Catchpoll's Cockscomb Captain Crackskull cracked?

DAVY DOLLDRUM dreamed he drove a Dragon:
Did Davy Dolldrum dream he drove a Dragon?

If Davy Dolldrum dreamed he drove a Dragon,
Where's the Dragon Davy Dolldrum dreamed he drove?

ENOCH ELKRIG ate
An empty Eggshell:
Did Enoch Elkrig eat
An empty Eggshell?
If Enoch Elkrig ate
An empty Eggshell,
Where's
The empty Eggshell
Enoch Elkrig ate?

FRANCIS FRIBBLE figured on a Frenchman's Filly:
Did Francis Fribble figure on a Frenchman's Filly?
If Francis Fribble figured on a Frenchman's Filly,
Where's the Frenchman's Filly Francis Fribble figured on?

GAFFER GILPIN got a Goose and Gander:
Did Gaffer Gilpin get a Goose and Gander?
If Gaffer Gilpin got a Goose and Gander,
Where's the Goose and Gander Gaffer Gilpin got?

HUMPHREY HUNCHBACK had a Hundred Hedgehogs:
Did Humphrey Hunchback have a Hundred Hedgehogs?
If Humphrey Hunchback had a Hundred Hedgehogs,
Where's the Hundred Hedgehogs Humphrey Hunchback had?

INIGO IMPEY itched for an Indian Image:

Did Inigo Impey itch for an Indian Image?

If Inigo Impey itched for an Indian Image,

Where's the Indian Image Inigo Impey itched for?

JUMPING JACKEY jeered a jesting Juggler:
Did Jumping Jackey jeer a jesting Juggler?
If Jumping Jackey jeered a jesting Juggler,
Where's the jesting Juggler Jumping Jackey jeered?

KIMBO KEMBLE kicked his Kinsman's Kettle:
Did Kimbo Kemble kick his Kinsman's Kettle?
If Kimbo Kemble kicked his Kinsman's Kettle,
Where's the Kinsman's Kettle Kimbo Kemble kicked?

LANKY LAWRENCE lost his Lass and Lobster:
Did Lanky Lawrence lose his Lass and Lobster?

If Lanky Lawrence lost his Lass and Lobster,
Where are the Lass and Lobster Lanky Lawrence lost?

MATTHEW MENDLEGS missed a mangled Monkey:

Did Matthew Mendlegs miss a mangled Monkey?

If Matthew Mendlegs missed a mangled Monkey,

Where's the mangled Monkey Matthew Mendlegs missed?

NEDDY NOODLE nipped his Neighbor's Nutmegs:
Did Neddy Noodle nip his Neighbor's Nutmegs?
If Neddy Noodle nipped his Neighbor's Nutmegs,
Where are the Neighbor's Nutmegs Neddy Noodle nipped?

OLIVER OGLETHORPE ogled an Owl and Oyster:
Did Oliver Oglethorpe ogle an Owl and Oyster?
If Oliver Oglethorpe ogled an Owl and Oyster,
Where are the Owl and Oyster Oliver Oglethorpe ogled?

PETER PIPER picked a peck of Pickled Peppers:

Did Peter Piper pick a peck of Pickled Peppers?

If Peter Piper picked a peck of Pickled Peppers,

Where's the peck of Pickled Peppers Peter Piper picked?

QUIXOTE QUICKSIGHT quizzed a queerish Quidbox:
Did Quixote Quicksight quiz a queerish Quidbox?
If Quixote Quicksight quizzed a queerish Quidbox,
Where's the queerish Quidbox Quixote Quicksight quizzed?

 RORY RUMPUS rode a raw-boned Racer:
Did Rory Rumpus ride a raw-boned Racer?
If Rory Rumpus rode a raw-boned Racer,
Where's the raw-boned Racer Rory Rumpus rode?

SAMMY SMELLIE smelt a Smell of Smallcoal:
Did Sammy Smellie smell a Smell of Smallcoal?
If Sammy Smellie smelt a Smell of Smallcoal,
Where's the Smell of Smallcoal Sammy Smellie smelt?

TIP-TOE TOMMY turned a Turk for Two-pence:
Did Tip-Toe Tommy turn a Turk for Two-pence?
If Tip-Toe Tommy turned a Turk for Two-pence,
Where's the Turk for Two-pence Tip-Toe Tommy turned?

UNCLE'S USHER urged an ugly Urchin:
Did Uncle's Usher urge an ugly Urchin?
If Uncle's Usher urged an ugly Urchin,
Where's the ugly Urchin Uncle's Usher urged?

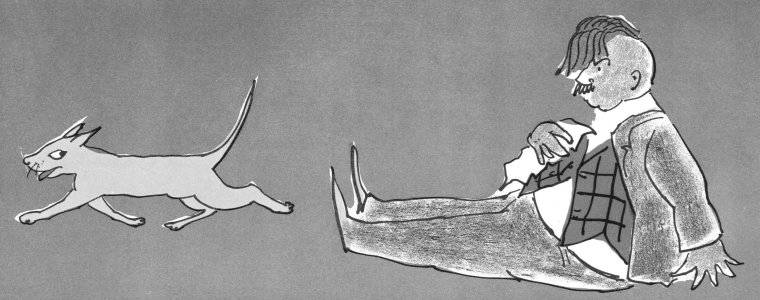

VILLIAM VEEDON viped his Vig and Vaistcoat:

Did Villiam Veedon vipe his Vig and Vaistcoat?

If Villiam Veedon viped his Vig and Vaistcoat,

Where are the Vig and Vaistcoat Villiam Veedon viped?

WALTER WADDLE won a walking Wager:
Did Walter Waddle win a walking Wager?
If Walter Waddle won a walking Wager,
Where's the walking Wager Walter Waddle won?

X Y Z have made my brains to crack-o:
X smokes, Y snuffs, and Z chews tobacco;
Yet oft by X Y Z much learning's taught,
But Peter Piper beats them all to nought.

A B C D E F G H I J K L M N O P Q R S T U V W X Y Z

PETER PIPER'S ALPHABET,
from which this text was taken, was first published by J.
Harris, St. Paul's Churchyard, London, in 1813. The first
American edition was published by Carter Andrews and
Company, Lancaster, Massachusetts, in 1830. The Harris
edition bore on the title page "Peter Piper's Practical Prin-
ciples of Plain and Perfect Pronunciation." The *Preface*
occurs on the back of the title page of the edition published
by Willard Johnson, 141 South Street, Philadelphia, 1836.